Contents

The restless Earth

For most of us, the Earth on which we live seems safe and secure. But some parts of the Earth are far from safe. There are places where, from time to time, the Earth rocks violently as an earthquake occurs. Elsewhere, molten rock, ashes, smoke and gases pour out from volcanoes. These things may happen with little or no warning.

People have always been frightened by earthquakes and volcanoes. The ancient Romans thought that one of their gods, Vulcan, lived inside a volcano. Vulcan was blacksmith to the gods. When smoke and flames poured from a volcano, the Romans thought that Vulcan was lighting his furnace. If the ground rumbled and shook they thought that Vulcan was hammering on his anvil.

The ancient Greeks believed that one of their gods, Poseidon, caused earthquakes. Poseidon was said to

An old Hindu idea of our Earth, and (below) Poseidon stamping the ground

look like a giant bull. When he was angry, Poseidon stamped the ground causing the Earth to shake. Some Hindus in India thought that the world stood on a golden plate. This in turn rested on the backs of elephants. If the elephants moved, the Earth shook, causing an earthquake.

Inside the Earth

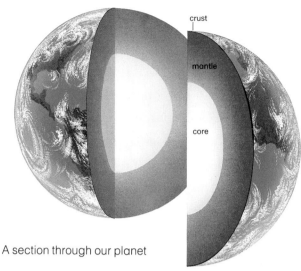

A section through our planet

Scientists have learned much about the inside of the Earth by studying earthquakes and volcanoes. We now know that the Earth is made up of layers. The outside of the Earth is covered by a layer of rocks and soil. This is the part of the Earth we live on. It is known as the Earth's crust. This crust of rocks goes underneath the oceans and seas as well.

Mines are deep holes in the Earth's crust. Deep down in mines it is very hot. The deeper you go down through the Earth's crust, the hotter it is. This is because underneath the crust is a thick layer of hotter, heavier rocks. This layer is known as the mantle. Parts of it are so hot that the rocks have melted and flow like treacle.

There are two more layers underneath the mantle. Together these form what is known as the Earth's core. The inner core is believed to be a solid ball of hot metal made up of iron and nickel. Around this inner core is the outer core consisting of iron and nickel which are so hot that they are a liquid.

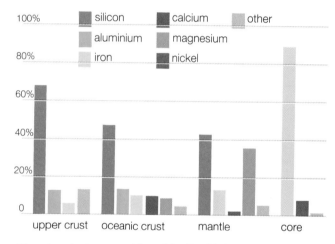

The chemical composition of the Earth's layers

Underneath a volcano

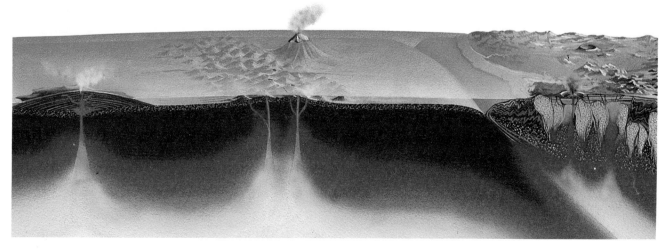

Faults and folds

Although most rocks are hard and strong, they will still bend and even break. Like the branches of a tree, rocks will bend to a certain extent. But if they are bent too far, they break.

If you look at cliffs or at the sides of a quarry you can sometimes see where the rocks have bent. These bends in the rocks are known as folds. Folds show where movements of the Earth's crust have bent the rocks. Sometimes huge movements of the Earth's crust fold rock layers into giant wrinkles. The mountains formed are known as fold mountains. Most of the big mountain ranges are fold mountains like this. They include the Himalayas, the Alps, the Andes and the Appalachian mountains.

The Awatere fault line, New Zealand

Folds in the rocks at Stair Hole, Dorset

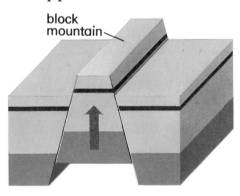

The formation of block mountains and rift valleys between two faults

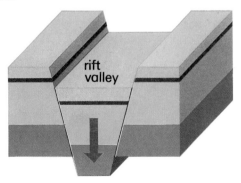

When the rocks bend they may crack or break. These cracks and breaks in the rocks are called faults. In places parallel faults have opened up in the rocks. Huge pressures later forced up a block of land between two of these faults. The mountains formed are called block mountains. The Vosges Mountains of France and the Black Forest region of Germany were formed like this. Sometimes a block of land slips down between two faults. This produces a rift valley. A huge rift valley runs for nearly 6,500 kilometres along Africa.

6

The crust of the Earth

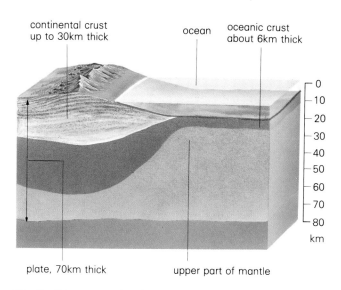

continental crust up to 30km thick

ocean

oceanic crust about 6km thick

0
10
20
30
40
50
60
70
80
km

plate, 70km thick

upper part of mantle

The Earth's crust under the sea and under a continent

The Earth's crust is not all the same thickness. On the continents beneath mountains, the crust may be 30 kilometres thick. Under the oceans it is only about 6 kilometres thick.

Nor is the Earth's crust just one huge sheet of rock. It does not cover the Earth like the skin of an orange.

In fact the Earth's crust is cracked and broken into at least 15 pieces. These pieces are called plates. Some of these plates have oceans on them. Other plates carry continents.

The plates are not still. They are being slowly pushed and pulled around by movements of the hot mantle rock below them. It is believed that millions of years ago all seven continents were joined together. Scientists have named this super-continent Pangaea. It is believed that Pangaea gradually broke up. The pieces drifted away from each other. They formed the seven continents we know today. But the continents haven't stopped moving. They are travelling very very slowly. It is mainly the movements of the Earth's continents and plates which cause earthquakes and volcanoes.

Pangaea very slowly broke up into today's continents

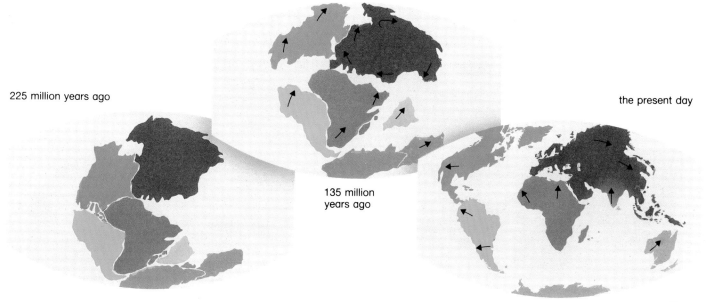

225 million years ago

135 million years ago

the present day

7

Drifting continents

The Modi Khola gorge in the Himalayas, Nepal

As we have seen, the continents are moving slowly. North America and Europe are slowly drifting apart. Each year the Atlantic Ocean becomes 2 or 3 centimetres wider. North America and Europe are drifting apart because a gap keeps opening up between the plates bearing these two continents. Liquid rock seeps up from the mantle through the gap in the floor of the Atlantic Ocean. This liquid rock hardens and keeps filling the gap formed between the two plates. And so a new strip of crust is always being formed under the Atlantic.

In other parts of the world, the Earth's crust is being drawn down into the mantle. In the eastern part of the Pacific Ocean, for example, a narrow strip of the Earth's crust is being sucked down inside the mantle. The loss of crust here makes up for that gained in other parts of the Pacific and Atlantic Oceans.

Where two of the Earth's plates collide, they push up fold mountains. The highest mountains in the world are the Himalayas. They were pushed up when India and Asia collided with each other millions of years ago. Fossil seashells have been found in rocks high up in the Himalayas. This shows that these rocks were once under the sea.

North America and Europe are drifting apart,

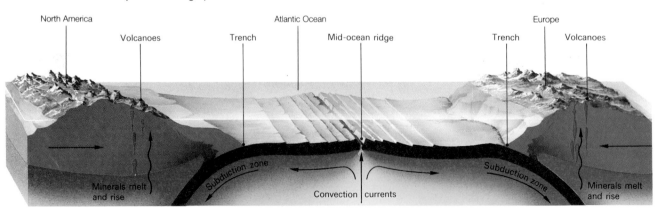

How earthquakes are caused

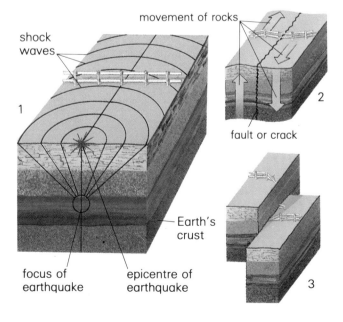

shock waves

movement of rocks

1

2

fault or crack

Earth's crust

focus of earthquake

epicentre of earthquake

3

The Earth's plates are always moving. Earthquakes are caused by movements of these plates. One plate sometimes sticks against another. Often this puts such a great strain on the rocks that they bend. The rocks may also split, forming a fault. Suddenly the two plates jerk apart. They usually give way along a fault. As the plates slip apart, the land above shudders and shakes. These jerky movements of the Earth's crust are called shocks or tremors.

In some ways an earthquake is rather like a drawer which doesn't slide smoothly on its runners. Pulling the drawer seems to have no effect. But suddenly the drawer gives way with a thump. It may even scatter the things inside.

Each year about 500,000 earthquakes are recorded. Most of these can only be recorded by delicate instruments. Stronger earthquakes may frighten people, make tree leaves shake and church bells ring. Every year about 1000 earthquakes are strong enough to cause damage. As a result of these, roads and railway tracks may buckle and twist. Sewers, gas and water pipes and electricity cables break. Buildings crack and fall down. In the worst earthquakes whole towns may be destroyed. And many people may be killed or injured.

Top: Earthquake damage in California.
Middle: After an earthquake in Chile.
Bottom: What causes an earthquake.

9

Where earthquakes happen

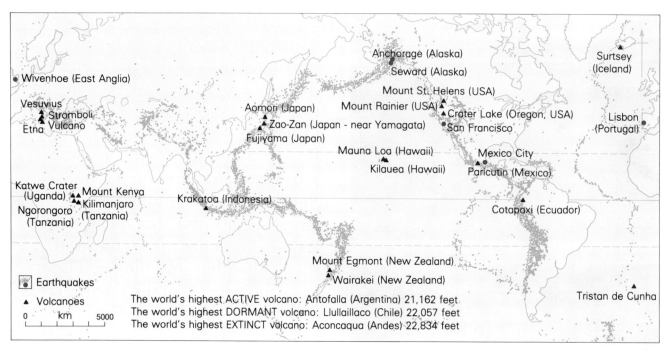

The earthquakes and volcanoes mentioned in this book

It is not possible to say when earthquakes are going to happen. But we do know where they are most likely to occur. This is because earthquakes mainly occur in definite bands around the world. These are the places where the Earth's plates meet each other. You can see the places where most earthquakes happen on the map on this page.

One of the main earthquake zones runs through the Mediterranean sea and across southern Asia. Another goes round the Pacific Ocean from New Zealand up to Japan. Then it passes down the west coast of North and South America. Earthquakes can occur outside these zones. But they are usually very mild. Most of the tremors are no worse than the vibrations caused by a large lorry. Very occasionally earthquakes like this happen in Britain.

The biggest earthquake recorded in Britain was the East Anglian earthquake of 1884. It damaged 1200 buildings. One person is believed to have been killed. Another big earthquake occurred in Britain in 1984. But no one was killed or badly injured. Serious earthquakes are very rare outside the main earthquake zones.

Rebuilding after the earthquake at Wivenhoe, East Anglia 1884

The San Andreas fault

Earthquake damage in a Californian supermarket

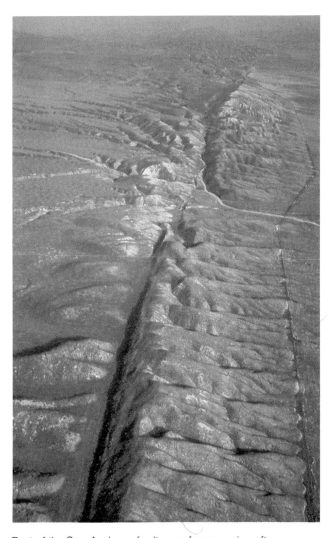

Part of the San Andreas fault seen from an aircraft

Most of the joints between the Earth's plates are under the oceans and seas. But along the western side of the United States one of these joints is on land. It is known as the San Andreas fault. This huge crack in the rocks runs for nearly 965 kilometres through California.

There are frequent slight earth tremors along the San Andreas fault. Occasionally there are severe earthquakes. All of these things happen because two of the Earth's plates are grinding against each other. One of the plates is fairly steady. But the other, the Pacific plate, is trying to move northwards. Mostly the plate moves about 5 centimetres a year. But during the San Francisco earthquake of 1906, the ground moved 5 metres in just one minute. The earthquake not only flattened the city of San Francisco, it also caused the deaths of over 700 people.

Another big earthquake could happen along the San Andreas fault at any time. It will happen if the fault makes another large, jerky movement. To try to stop this, scientists have been pumping millions of litres of water into old mines in the area around the fault. They hope the water will allow the rocks to slide over each other more easily.

Tsunamis

Tsunamis may cause serious flooding and damage

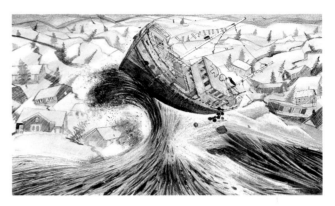

Vibrations come from the earthquake's epicentre

The vibrations from an earthquake are most violent near the fault which caused it. The exact spot on the Earth's surface above the place where an earthquake occurs is called its epicentre (see page 9). The vibrations spread out from the epicentre of the earthquake. The vibrations rarely last for more than a minute or two. They spread out through the Earth rather like the ripples made by a stone thrown into a pond.

When an earthquake occurs under the sea, the vibrations may throw the water up into great waves. These are often called tidal waves or tsunamis. In the open sea a tsunami may be quite small. The waves are often only a metre or so high. Such waves are hardly noticeable. But tsunamis can travel huge distances. And they move at great speed. Tsunamis can reach speeds of 600 to 800 km per hour.

In the shallow water around the coasts and in narrow inlets, the waves grow to be enormous. They may be 60 metres high. Such large

tsunamis cause serious flooding and immense damage. Tsunamis are also caused by the eruptions of volcanoes under the sea.

Tsunami wreckage in Seward, Alaska 1964

Earthquake disasters

After an earthquake in Anchorage, Alaska 1964

Millions of people around the world have been killed during earthquakes. China has perhaps suffered the most. An earthquake in 1556 is said to have killed 830,000 people. Another earthquake in China in 1976 killed 242,000 people.

There have also been many earthquakes in Japan. One in 1923 killed more than 140,000 people. Countless buildings were destroyed, many by fires started when cooking stoves tipped over.

In 1737 an earthquake in India killed 300,000 people. Italy, Iran and Portugal have also suffered badly. At Lisbon in Portugal, three great earthquakes occurred on the same day in 1755. Churches, palaces, houses and shops shook and then tumbled. The tremors were felt as far away as Scotland, Norway and Sweden. Tsunamis as high as houses rolled in from the sea, causing more damage. Altogether about 30,000 people were killed.

Chaos after the Mexican earthquake of 1985

The San Francisco earthquake

1906 – California Street in San Francisco after the 'quake'

Most people were asleep on the morning of 18th April 1906 when the San Francisco earthquake began. It was just 5.13 a.m. when, without any warning, the whole city started to rock violently. At first the buildings shook, then they fell apart. Great cracks appeared in the ground. Many people thought the end of the world had come. And then suddenly all was still and quiet again.

The earthquake had lasted just 48 seconds. But the worst horror was yet to come. Fires broke out all over the city. With water mains broken and streets littered with rubble, firemen had great difficulty fighting the fires. Many of the wooden houses which had withstood the earthquake now blazed. The fires did even more damage than the earthquake. They burned for three days. Eventually heavy rain put the fires out.

The earthquake and fires had left over 700 people dead and a quarter of a million people homeless. About 28,000 buildings in the centre of the city had been destroyed. And as we saw on page 11, another earthquake disaster could strike San Francisco at any time.

Preventing earthquake damage

Above: Modern earthquake-proof skyscrapers in Tokyo, Japan Below: Wide city streets in Sapporo, Japan

Earthquakes occur with little or no warning. But some birds and animals seem to know hours, sometimes days before, that an earthquake is going to happen. By studying these it may be possible in the future to warn people of the danger of an earthquake.

It is also possible to make buildings less liable to earthquake damage. When the Japanese earthquake struck in 1923, skyscrapers remained standing while ordinary buildings fell. This was because the skycrapers had steel frames. These were able to sway as the earthquake tremors passed them.

Nowadays in earthquake zones, new buildings are placed on solid rocks. They have a framework of strong flexible steel. There are few doors and windows. Sometimes the roofs are covered with rubber or plastic pads instead of tiles. The streets are made wide so that buildings will not block them if they fall. Open spaces are left in towns. People can go to these out of reach of falling buildings.

Volcanoes

Like earthquakes, volcanoes are among the most powerful forces in nature. A volcano is a hole in the Earth's crust. From this opening molten rock, smoke and gases escape from the Earth's mantle. The molten rock which comes from a volcano is known as lava.

When lava comes from a volcano, we say the volcano is erupting. Some kinds of lava are thick and sticky. They solidify quickly. Sometimes they solidify inside the opening of the volcano and stop it erupting. However gases in the lava build up the pressure underneath this plug of rock. Eventually the pressure may build up enough to blast away the plug with an explosion. Lumps of solid rock are hurled into the sky. Blobs of lava and cinders rain down on the surrounding countryside. And the sky may darken with clouds of smoke, ash and dust. This kind of volcanic eruption is the most violent.

Other kinds of lava are very thin and runny. They can flow for many kilometres before they solidify. This kind of volcanic eruption is much less violent.

Top: Flowing lava pours into the sea

Middle: This farm is about to be engulfed in lava

Bottom: A famous volcano – Mount St. Helens, exploding at 1.00pm, May 18, 1980, Washington State, USA

There are about 500 active volcanoes in the world. Like earthquakes, volcanoes are found where there are weak places, or faults, in the Earth's crust (see page 10). Usually this is where two of the Earth's plates crash together or separate. Volcanoes and earthquakes occur in the same general areas. But the worst earthquakes take place where there are no volcanoes. Possibly the volcanoes relieve the pressures of the molten rocks and hot gases of the Earth's mantle.

There is a band of weak places or faults around the edge of the Pacific Ocean. Most of the world's active volcanoes are found there. These volcanoes make up what is sometimes called the Pacific Ring of Fire. There is another band of volcanoes along a line of weakness in the Atlantic Ocean. They include volcanoes in Iceland, the Azores, the Canary Islands and the island of Tristan da Cunha. Four of the world's most famous volcanoes lie around the edges of the Mediterranean Sea. They are Etna, Vesuvius, Stromboli and Vulcano.

Many of the islands of the Pacific Ocean are the tops of undersea volcanoes. They grew bigger until they appeared above the surface of the water.

Smoke, ash, lava, fire and dust

Dormant and extinct volcanoes

Fujiyama and a fishing festival boat

Mount Rainier, Seattle, Washington State, USA

When a volcano has not erupted for a very long time, it is said to be dormant. The word dormant means 'sleeping'. Normally volcanoes erupt for a short time. Then they remain dormant for a long period. Fujiyama in Japan is a dormant volcano. It last erupted in 1707. Mount Rainier in the United States last erupted over 100 years ago.

While a volcano is dormant, steam may come from it. This is true of both Fujiyama and Mount Rainier. Lava may bubble in the crater of the volcano. Sometimes the lava hardens. This solid lava may stop the volcano from erupting any more. This happened with Mount Kenya. More often, though, it means that when the volcano does next erupt it will explode into life. Krakatoa in Indonesia was a volcano which exploded in this way.

The extinct shield volcano – Kilimanjaro – and impala

If a volcano has shown no signs of life for thousands of years it is said to be extinct. Two famous extinct volcanoes are Mount Egmont in New Zealand and Kilimanjaro in Tanzania. There are also many extinct volcanoes in the British Isles, France and Germany.

Of course it is not easy to tell when a volcano is dormant and when it is extinct. Everyone thought that the volcano on Tristan da Cunha was extinct, until it erupted in 1961. Evidently the volcano was not extinct, it was only dormant.

Do you remember?

1 What is the Earth's crust?

2 What would you notice as you went deeper and deeper down a mine?

3 What is the mantle like?

4 How do the inner and outer cores of the Earth differ?

5 What are bends in the Earth's rocks called?

6 Name two ranges of mountains which were formed by folding of the Earth's crust.

7 How is a rift valley formed?

8 What are the Earth's plates?

9 How many plates are there?

10 What makes the Earth's plates move?

11 How did fossil seashells get to be high up in the Himalayan mountains?

12 What is the super-continent called which was formed when the seven continents were joined together?

13 Why are the continents of North America and Europe slowly moving apart?

14 What is happening on the sea-bed between North America and Europe?

15 What do we call it when rocks crack or break?

16 How are earthquakes caused?

17 Roughly how many earthquakes are recorded each year?

18 Where do most earthquakes occur?

19 Where is the San Andreas Fault?

20 What are scientists doing to try to prevent earthquakes along the San Andreas Fault?

21 What is the exact centre of an earthquake called?

22 How do the vibrations from an earthquake spread out?

23 What is a tsunami?

24 Name four countries where earthquakes often occur.

25 What can be done to make buildings safer in an earthquake?

26 What is lava?

27 What do we say is happening when lava comes from a volcano?

28 Whereabouts are most of the world's active volcanoes found?

29 What is a dormant volcano?

30 What is an extinct volcano?

Things to do

1 A model of the centre of the Earth Use different coloured pieces of plasticine to make a model of a section through the Earth (see page 5). On your model show the inner and outer cores, the mantle and the Earth's crust.

2 Write a story Write a story called 'Journey to the centre of the Earth'.

3 A model of Pangaea Obtain or draw a small map of the world. Stick your map onto a thin sheet of polystyrene plastic, such as a polystyrene ceiling tile. Use a sharp knife (Careful!) to cut out the seven continents. Arrange them together so that they form a model of Pangaea (see page 7). Which continent had to move the greatest distance to reach its present position? Which continent had to move from a warm or hot climate to a very cold one?

4 Folding Obtain some thin card or sheets of paper. Use pieces all the same size but of different colours. Lay the pieces of card or paper evenly between your hands and move your hands together so that the paper or card sags downwards. Then put the paper or card on a table and move your hands together so that paper or card arches upwards. This is the way layers of rock are folded by pressures of the Earth's crust. You can do the same experiment using P.E. mats in the gym.

Make models of folds and faults using clay or plasticine.

5 The Rift Valley On page 6, we saw how a rift valley is formed. Pretend that you were standing on the land which is now at the bottom of Africa's Rift Valley when the valley was formed. Write a story describing your adventures.

6 A model earthquake Make a model earthquake. Find two planks of wood both the same thickness. Lay them side by side. Use Lego or some other building blocks to make model houses. Place these across your 'fault'. Move the two planks quickly either horizontally, vertically or both. Watch your buildings topple.

Can you make model buildings which will withstand a small model earthquake?

7 Experiment with vibrations As we saw on page 12, during an earthquake shock waves or vibrations pass through the ground. Make your own vibrations. Thump the end of a long table with your hand while a friend puts his hand on the table. Can your friend feel the vibration one metre away? How far away must he be if he is not to feel the vibration?

Stand empty matchboxes or dominoes on end in a row across the table. Bang the table with your fist. Does your 'earthquake' make the matchboxes or dominoes topple over? Is it easier to make the matchboxes or dominoes topple when they are near to your fist or further away?

8 Preparing for an earthquake disaster Pretend that earthquakes are common where you live. Work with a group of friends and make plans for dealing with a severe earthquake. Decide how you would:

(a) Deal with the injured
(b) Find shelter for the homeless
(c) Deal with dangerous buildings
(d) Put out fires
(e) Provide food and water for the survivors.

Decide what help you will need to carry out your plans. How will you contact helpers since the telephone service may be destroyed in the earthquake? Which buildings are most likely to remain standing during an earthquake? Which of these will you use as your headquarters?

Write out your plan of action for dealing with an earthquake disaster. Prepare a poster to warn people what they should do if an earthquake occurs.

9 A model tsunami Stand a brick in the middle of a large bowl or baby bath. Fill the bowl or bath with water until it reaches to within a centimetre of the top of the bath.

Use matchboxes to make a model village on the top of the brick. Now use your hands to make a miniature tsunami in the bath or bowl. What happens to the model village?

10 Collect stamps Make a collection of postage stamps which show pictures of volcanoes. Display your stamps in an album or on a wallchart. Write a sentence or two about each of the stamps, the volcanoes they show, and the countries the stamps came from.

11 A model of the Earth's plates Obtain or draw a small map of the world. Mark on it the edges of the Earth's plates. Stick your map onto a thin sheet of polystyrene plastic (a polystyrene ceiling tile will do very well). Use a sharp knife (*Careful!*) to cut out the plates. Experiment to see what will happen to, say, the Pacific Ocean if the Atlantic becomes wider. What countries will move? What will happen if Africa moves closer to Europe?

12 A volcano in the city Write a story describing the changes which might take place if a volcano erupted in the centre of London or Paris.

13 Keep a scrapbook Cut out newspaper articles and pictures which describe earthquakes and volcanic eruptions that occur over the next year. Make a scrapbook with your newspaper cuttings. Plot the positions of the earthquakes and volcanoes on a small map of the world. Stick that in your scrapbook as well. Keep a note of the amount of damage caused by the earthquakes and volcanoes.

14 Make a collage Make a collage by using cut-out pictures to make one large interesting picture about volcanoes and the people, plants and animals that live near them.

15 Draw a graph of volcanoes Find out the heights of some volcanoes. Draw a graph to show their heights. The graph below shows the heights of some of the world's highest mountains. Model your graph on this.

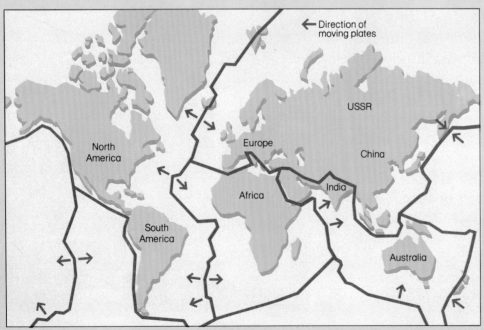

Things to find out

1 Look at the map on page 10, showing where most earthquakes occur. Now study an atlas. Make a list of ten cities with a population of one million or more which are in the areas where earthquakes are likely to occur.

2 How is it that scientists know so much about the centre of the Earth, even though no one has even drilled down so far as the mantle?

3 Scientists use an instrument called a seismometer to measure the strengths of earthquakes. Find out how a seismometer works. What scale of measurements is used for the strengths of earthquakes?

4 Make a list of all the things people use rocks for. How many things can you think of?

5 Try to find out whether there are earthquakes (moonquakes) or volcanoes on the moon.

6 How are landslides and avalanches different from an earthquake? Find out where landslides and avalanches occur.

7 Find out which country has the most active volcanoes.

8 Here are the names of some famous volcanoes: Mont Pelée, Krakatoa, Mauna Loa, Fujiyama, Mount Etna, Mayon, Mount Erebus, Ruapehu. They are all to be found on islands. Find out the name of the island or island group to which each volcano belongs.

9 What would be the effect of seawater reaching the hot lava from a volcano? How could this happen?

10 Look in travel agents' brochures and advertisements and find out which areas with active or dormant volcanoes are most often visited by tourists.

11 Sometimes after a big volcanic eruption there may be spectacular sunsets. The summers may be cooler and wetter and the winters colder. Find out what causes these changes in the weather.

12 Here is a map quiz. An atlas will help you to answer these questions about the map below:
(a) The map shows part of a sea which is almost completely surrounded by land. What is the name of this sea?
(b) What is the name of the country which is shaped rather like a boot?
(c) What is the name of the volcano labelled A?
(d) What is the name of the island labelled B?
(e) What is the name of the volcano on the island labelled B?
(f) What is the name of the volcano on the tiny island labelled C?
(g) There is another volcano on the tiny island labelled D. What is its name?
(h) Of the four volcanoes marked on this map, which is the tallest?

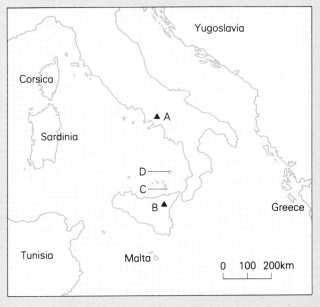

The shapes of volcanoes

Sections through (top) a stratavolcano and (bottom) a shield volcano

All volcanoes begin life as a crack or hole in the ground. As the volcano erupts, lava and ash pile up around this crack or hole. They gradually build up into a hill or mountain. This is called the cone of the volcano.

But not all volcanoes are the same shape. If runny lava comes from the volcano, this may flow a long way before it hardens. The volcano it forms has gently sloping sides. Such a volcano is known as a shield volcano. This is because it is shaped like an upturned shield. Diamond Head and Mauna Loa in Hawaii are good examples of shield volcanoes.

If the lava is sticky it hardens quickly. It builds up a volcano with steep sides. The cones of most volcanoes are made up of layers of ash and cinders, and layers of lava. These are known as composite cones or stratovolcanoes. Cotopaxi in Ecuador and Fujiyama in Japan are stratovolcanoes.

At the top of the volcano is a deep hollow. This is called its crater. When the volcano erupts, smoke, flames and lava shoot out of the crater. As time goes by, other openings may appear on the sides of the volcano. Lava and smoke may come from these openings as well and cause further hazards.

24

Volcanoes in the sea

Mauna Loa volcano, Hawaii

Kilauea – fountains and ribbons of lava

The Hawaiian Islands are a group of more than 100 islands in the Pacific Ocean. They are actually the tips of undersea mountains. All of the islands were formed by volcanoes. One of the islands, Hawaii, is the top of a mountain more than 9,150 metres high. This is higher than Mount Everest.

Hawaii is made up of several volcanoes. One of them, Mauna Loa, is the largest active volcano in the world. Mauna Loa is a shield volcano. Its top is like a huge upturned saucer.

Mauna Loa erupts on average about once every 3 to 4 years. Its lava is very thin and runny. When the volcano erupts, the lava flows huge distances before it cools and hardens. That is why Mauna Loa has such gently sloping sides. At its top or summit, Mauna Loa has a huge oval crater. But as well as erupting from this, Mauna Loa often erupts from cracks in its sides. Mauna Loa and its neighbouring volcano Kilauea are visited by many tourists. Visitors can drive right to the rim of the volcanoes and look down into their craters.

Sightseers at a volcano

Geysers and hot springs

A geyser is a spring. But unlike ordinary springs, the water which comes out of a geyser is scalding hot. The water doesn't flow continuously, it comes out in spurts. Geysers are found in many volcanic areas of the world. They are particularly common in Iceland and on New Zealand's North Island. There are also geysers in the state of Wyoming in the United States.

A geyser consists of a hole in the ground. This hole goes deep into the ground to where the rocks are hot. Rain water seeps through the ground until it touches the hot rocks. The water is heated. Eventually hot water and steam are shot up into the air through the hole. Soon more water seeps into the hole. When this is heated up, the geyser is ready for the next eruption.

Some geysers throw water and steam hundreds of metres into the air. They may erupt at regular intervals. One geyser at Wyoming in the United States is called 'Old Faithful'. It erupts every hour for about 5 minutes. It has been doing this for hundreds of years.

The water in geysers usually contains a lot of dissolved chemicals. Often these collect around the opening of the geyser. Around some geysers there are also pools of bubbling, boiling mud.

Top: A hot spring in Iceland
Middle: 'Old Faithful' geyser
Bottom: Mud spring in Rotorua, New Zealand

Krakatoa

Krakatoa in Indonesia

The world's greatest explosion was caused by a volcano. This volcano was Krakatoa, an island in Indonesia. Krakatoa had been quiet for more than 200 years. A plug of solid lava had blocked its opening. But unbeknown to everyone, gases were collecting beneath the plug. One day in August 1883, the pressure of these gases became so great that Krakatoa exploded.

The explosion destroyed two-thirds of the island. It was so loud that it was heard clearly 5,000 kilometres away. Rocks were thrown 55 kilometres high into the air. Clouds of dust caused darkness for days.

Only a few people were killed by the explosion of Krakatoa. But it rocked the sea-bed, creating a huge wave. This giant tsunami swamped nearby islands. In places the wave was over 35 metres high. It destroyed a total of 163 villages. And more than 36,000 people were drowned.

Great clouds of dust from Krakatoa gradually drifted around the world. For the next three years this dust scattered the sun's rays. It caused spectacular sunsets every-where. And the world had a series of cool summers and freezing winters.

Thousands drowned after the 1883 eruption

Vesuvius

The crater of Vesuvius

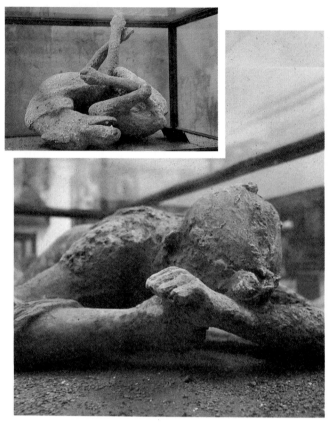

Victims of Pompeii were buried in ash nearly 2,000 years ago; the dog was chained and couldn't escape

Vesuvius is one of the world's most famous volcanoes. It is on the southern coast of Italy behind the city of Naples. Vesuvius is the only active volcano on the mainland of Europe. There are, however, other active volcanoes on nearby islands.

From time to time Vesuvius erupts violently. The last time was in 1944. However, Vesuvius' most famous eruption was in AD 79. The volcano had been quiet for many centuries. Suddenly there was an enormous explosion. The top of Vesuvius blew off. Huge quantities of ash showered down on the surrounding plain.

The city of Pompeii was buried by this ash. In places the ash was 6 metres deep. A nearby town, Herculaneum, was buried by molten lava. Thousands of people were killed. At Pompeii the shapes of their bodies were preserved in the ash. In more recent times, the shapes of the people have been filled with plaster of Paris so that they show up clearly. And the ash has been cleared. Now visitors can walk the streets and see Pompeii as it was in AD 79 on the day Vesuvius erupted.

Ruined Pompeii today

Mount Etna

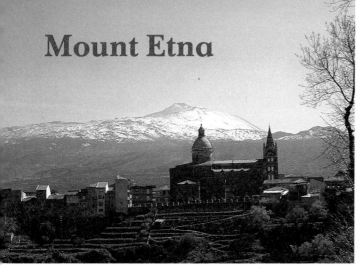

Above: Etna from Randazzo. Below: Etna erupting

Lava flow from Etna

Mount Etna is the largest volcano in Europe. It lies on the island of Sicily in the Mediterranean Sea. At present Mount Etna is 3260 metres high, and its top is often snow-covered. But Etna is not a simple volcano and its height changes from time to time. On its main cone there are hundreds of smaller cones and craters. Like Vesuvius, Etna always shows some signs of life. In the last 2,500 years, Etna has erupted more than 400 times. The last time was in 1983.

On the lower slopes of Mount Etna there are orange and lemon groves. Higher up, grape vines are grown. Above the farming areas there are forests. Many people live on the slopes of Etna and work on these farms and forests.

During the 1983 eruption, streams of lava threatened the towns and villages below. To save their houses, the people dug a deep canal to carry the lava away from their homes. Then explosives were used to try to force the streams of lava into the canal. Unfortunately the results were only partly successful. And a number of houses and hotels were destroyed.

Red hot lava consumes everything in its path

Tristan de Cunha

Tristan de Cunha is probably the loneliest island in the world. It lies in the South Atlantic Ocean. The nearest mainland is the Cape of Good Hope, nearly 3000 kilometres away.

Tristan da Cunha is a volcano. Everyone thought it was extinct. But one day in October 1961 the volcano started rumbling and the ground trembled. Soon the noise grew louder. Suddenly huge cracks appeared in the sides of the volcano. Seconds later lava started streaming down towards the village below. The lava completely buried the island's fish-canning factory. Even a radio mast 20 metres high was covered. To escape, the people had to take to the sea in their boats. After a few days they were rescued and taken to England.

Two years later, when the volcano had stopped erupting, the islanders returned to their homes. Luckily the lava had stopped just short of the cottages. The people were able to go on living there again.

This lava 'field' tumbles straight into the sea

Smouldering rocks show that the volcano is still alive

30

Mount Erebus

Ice and steam of Mount Erebus

Even Antarctica, the coldest place on Earth, has some volcanoes. Most of them are extinct, though. Only Mount Erebus still actively erupts. Although Mount Erebus is surrounded by ice and snow, steam is pouring from it all the time.

Mount Erebus has one main crater and several smaller ones. Within the main crater is a large lake. But this lake is not filled with water. It is filled with molten lava which bubbles and boils. Two or three times a day, lumps of lava shoot out of the smaller craters on Mount Erebus.

Near the top of the volcano there are geysers. From time to time hot water and steam spurt out from these. Elsewhere on Mount Erebus, hot gases escape into the bitterly cold Antarctic air. These hot gases have made caves in the ice on the volcano.

An ice tower on the side of the volcano

Lava lake inside the volcano

The birth of a volcano

Many people have seen a volcano erupting. But few have ever seen the birth of a new volcano. One person who did was a Mexican farmer from the village of Paricutin.

For some time a small crack in the farmer's cornfield had been growing longer. And then one afternoon in February 1943, the ground began to shake. The surface of the field around the crack rose. A hissing cloud of smoke, gases and ashes began to pour from the ground. The terrified farmer ran to safety.

By evening the cloud of smoke was much larger, and red-hot rocks were shooting into the air. The new volcano grew very rapidly. Within 24 hours the cornfield was covered by a cone of ashes 50 metres high. At the end of the week the cone had grown to about 150 metres.

The new volcano continued to erupt for another 8 years. By then the rim of its crater stood 410 metres above the remains of the cornfield.

Paricutin destroyed the village around this church

The cone of Paricutin volcano

Paricutin's volcano had destroyed two villages and hundreds of homes. But Paricutin is famous not because of the damage it did, but because it gave scientists a rare chance to study the growth of a new volcano.

The birth and growth of Paricutin

Surtsey – a new island

Surtsey erupting – November 1963

Surtsey – 20 years after its birth

When an undersea volcano erupts it may form an island. Until 1963 no one had actually seen one of these islands being formed. But in that year some fishermen off the coast of Iceland saw clouds of smoke rising from the sea. At first they thought a ship was on fire. When they got nearer the spot, the fishermen realised the smoke was coming from a volcano on the sea-bed.

Before long, steam, smoke and lumps of molten rock were being hurled 400 metres into the air. The next day the volcano had formed a small island. The volcano had built itself up above the surface of the sea. For several months the volcano continued to erupt. Scientists were able to watch the new island grow.

When the eruptions stopped, the island covered an area of 2.6 square kilometres. Its highest point was more than 170 metres above the sea. The island was named Surtsey after the old Icelandic god of fire. Only months after it was formed, the first seeds and young plants were found on Surtsey. They had either been carried there by the wind or been dropped by birds. Just four years after Surtsey was formed there were 23 species of birds living on it. There were also 22 kinds of insects and many different kinds of plants.

33

Ruins of a lost civilization on Crete, at Phaestos

Atlantis was a rich and powerful island civilisation. According to legend, Atlantis disappeared under the sea. This story was told by the Greek philosopher Plato in 360 BC, but the story was old then.

Various places have been suggested as the site for Atlantis. Some say it was on Crete or the neighbouring island of Santorini. There is evidence that on both these islands, people were living in large cities 17,000 years ago. At that time people in the rest of Europe were living in primitive villages. But sometime long ago, the civilisations on both Crete and Santorini disappeared.

In 1859 the remains of fine buildings were found 30 metres below ground on Crete. These may have been the remains of the lost civilisation. It has since been discovered there was a huge volcanic eruption on Santorini 3,500 years ago. The island was destroyed in the explosion. And the huge tsunami which resulted destroyed much of Crete. It may have been this tidal wave which gave rise to the story of Atlantis disappearing under the sea.

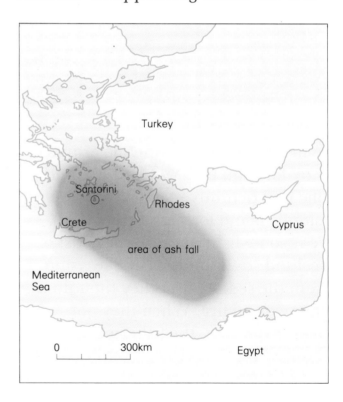

New rocks from volcanoes

When the lava from a volcano hardens, it forms rock. The rocks which come from volcanic lava are known as igneous rocks. Igneous means 'fire'. There are many different kinds of igneous rock.

If the lava from a volcano comes to the surface of the ground it cools quickly. If the molten rock collects in a cavity underground, it cools slowly. Beautiful shapes called crystals may form in the rock. Granite contains many large crystals. These were formed when molten rock cooled Beautiful shapes called crystals may form in the rock. Granite contains many large crystals. These were formed when volcanic lava cooled slowly. Granite is often used in buildings and, when broken up, for roads and motorways.

If gases are trapped in the lava as it cools, then pumice is formed. Pumice is very light and has thousands of bubbles of gas in it. It is sometimes used for rubbing down paintwork.

The heat from a volcano can also change existing rocks. Slate, which is used for roofs, was once soft shale. It was probably changed by the heat from a volcano and the pressure of other rocks. Similarly the beautiful rock marble was once limestone. A number of valuable minerals are found in igneous rocks. Diamonds, opals, agates and amethysts are just some of the mineral crystals, or gemstones, which are found in igneous rocks. So are many valuable metals such as gold, silver and platinum.

Some igneous rocks (top to bottom): basalt, andesite and granite

Gemstones from Zimbabwe

Volcanoes and the landscape

Above: The Giant's Causeway, Northern Ireland. Below left: Edinburgh Castle. Below right: The Puys Volcanic Chain, France.

Even in those parts of the world which have no active volcanoes, there are often extinct ones. In the British Isles, France and Germany, for example, there are no active volcanoes. But igneous rocks from old volcanoes are still common.

Granite is one of these igneous rocks. Granite hills and mountains are found in many parts of Britain, France and Germany. Some rocks in Northern Ireland are shaped like huge stepping stones. People once thought they were used by giants to get from Ireland to Scotland. They called these rocks the Giant's Causeway. We now know these strange rocks are made of basalt. They were formed long ago when lava from a volcano cooled. The castles at Edinburgh and Dumbarton are built on old volcanoes. So is the chapel at Le Puy in France.

One of the most unusual mountain ranges is the Puys Volcanic Chain in southern France. This consists of a series of 60 extinct volcanoes. They have all been worn down or eroded by the weather. But on most of them the craters can still be seen.

Craters and crater lakes

Panorama of the Crater Lake, Oregon, USA

Rather surprisingly, volcanoes can help to form some lakes. High in the mountains of Oregon in the United States of America is a deep blue lake. It is nearly circular and 9 kilometres across and 600 metres deep. The surrounding cliffs rise another 600 metres above the surface of the water. The lake is known as Crater Lake.

Although it sits on the top of an extinct volcano, Crater Lake is not actually a crater. The lake was formed when, after a series of eruptions, the sides of the volcano collapsed inwards. Rainwater soon filled the gaping hole. Mashu Lake in Japan was formed in a similar way.

Other crater lakes were formed when a huge explosion blew the top off a volcano. The Katwe Craters in Uganda, Africa, were formed like this. The proper name for one of these large cavities in the top of an extinct volcano is a caldera.

A storm clearing over the Ngorongoro crater in Tanzania

Not all calderas fill completely with water. One of the most famous calderas is the Ngorongoro Crater in Tanzania. This huge bowl is 20 kilometres across, but it is only partially filled with water. It is now a wildlife reserve and large herds of antelopes, gazelles and zebra roam across its dry grassy plains.

Crater of Zao-Zan, near Yamagata, Japan

37

Useful volcanoes

Although they are dangerous and destructive, volcanoes have their uses. There are many farms and even villages on the slopes of some volcanoes. This is because when the lava and ash turn into soil, that soil is sometimes very fertile and can be used for orchards or vineyards.

Another useful product from some volcanoes is hot water. This hot water comes from springs and geysers around volcanoes. In Iceland the water from hot springs is used to heat swimming pools and to centrally heat houses and flats. The water from the hot springs is also used to heat greenhouses. It means tomatoes, grapes and even tropical fruits like bananas can be grown. In several countries, hot water from volcanoes is used to make electricity. Pipes take the hot water to a power station. There it is used to produce steam which turns the generators. These are the machines which make electricity.

A useful chemical called sulphur is found near some volcanoes. Sulphur is used for hardening rubber tyres, and for making sulphuric acid, gunpowder and some ointments and medicines. And of course volcanoes are often a popular tourist attraction. Many tourists visit famous volcanoes such as Vesuvius, Fujiyama, Stromboli, Mount Etna and others.

Above: Vineyard on volcanic rock   Middle: Swimming pools built over natural steam sources in Reykjavik, Iceland Right: Steam power station, Wairakei, New Zealand

Do you remember

1 How does a volcano begin life?

2 What is the cone of a volcano?

3 What do we call a volcano which has gently sloping sides?

4 What is the lava like which forms volcanoes with gently sloping sides?

5 What is the cone of a stratovolcano made of?

6 What is the hollow in the top of a volcano called?

7 How were the Hawaiian Islands formed?

8 What kind of volcano is Mauna Loa?

9 Why does Mauna Loa have gently sloping sides?

10 What is a geyser?

11 Where are most geysers found?

12 What caused the world's greatest explosion?

13 What happened when a plug of solid lava formed in the opening of Krakatoa?

14 What effects did the dust from Krakatoa have?

15 In which country is the volcano Vesuvius?

16 How was Pompeii buried?

17 How were the shapes of the bodies of the people of Pompeii preserved?

18 Name three crops which are grown on Mount Etna.

19 What did the people of Sicily do to try to protect their homes from the lava coming from Mount Etna?

20 How did the people of Tristan da Cunha escape when the volcano erupted?

21 On which continent is the Mount Erebus volcano to be found?

22 What is the crater of Mount Erebus like?

23 Why is the volcano near the village of Paricutin famous?

24 Where is the island of Surtsey?

25 How was the island of Surtsey formed?

26 What was Atlantis?

27 What are igneous rocks?

28 What are the rocks like which are formed when lava from a volcano cools quickly?

29 How may crystals be formed in a rock?

30 In what ways can the hot water from around a volcano be useful?

Things to do

1 Make a model volcano.
Make the cone of the volcano with plasticine or plaster of Paris. Do not forget to make a hole in the top of the volcano for the crater.

Take a tuft of cotton wool. Paint it red, orange and black. Stick it in the crater of the volcano. The cotton wool can be the smoke and flames coming from the volcano.

2 Rock Quiz
Here is a picture of some more volcanic rocks: they are lava, pumice, obsidian and trachyte. Try to find out which is which.

3 Make a collection of rocks
Anyone can do this, not just those who live near mountains or volcanoes.

Look for pebbles and pieces of rock in the garden, at the seaside, by the roadside and in the country. River banks, the beds of streams, road cuttings, old quarries and building sites can also produce rock samples. These last places are *dangerous*, though. Do not go to them without permission, and *always* go with a grown-up.

Wash your rocks and pebbles carefully and dry them. Label each one with the name of the place where you found it and the date. Make a display of the rocks and pebbles for your friends to look at.

When you are searching for rock specimens, always keep a lookout for fossils. Make a collection of these as well. Carefully clean and wash each one. Label it saying where and when you found it.

Use books to try to find the names of your rocks and fossils. Try to find out how each kind of rock in your collection was formed.

4 Visit your local museum Look at their collection of rocks, minerals and fossils. How many of the rocks, minerals and fossils were found locally? How many came from volcanic areas?

You may be able to find out the names of some of your own rocks and fossils if you compare them with those in the museum's collection.

5 How hard are rocks? Look at some rocks or pebbles carefully, using a hand lens or a magnifying glass. What colour is each one? Is it rough or smooth to the touch? Does it appear to be made of grains? Is the specimen made of crystals?

Is the rock or pebble made up of all the same materials? Will the rock soak up water? Are there any fossils in it?

How hard or soft is each rock or pebble? One of the best ways to test for hardness is to try to scratch your rock with different things. Try your fingernail first. If you cannot scratch the rock with your fingernail, try to scratch it with a copper coin. Next, try to scratch the rock or pebble with the blade of a penknife or a screwdriver. *Careful!* If the rock still will not scratch, try a steel file.

If you have one, it is a good idea to fix your rock in the vice on a work-bench. Then you will not scratch or cut yourself when you see how hard or soft your rocks are. Try these tests on rocks made by people, such as brick or concrete, as well.

Make a table of your results like the one below. Which is the hardest rock, which is the softest?

6 Granite Granite is one kind of igneous rock. It is used a great deal as a facing for large buildings, and for gravestones and monuments. In some places granite is used for kerbstones.

Look carefully at all the different kinds of granite you can find. Can you see any crystals in the granite? What colour are they? What colour is the rest of the granite? If you can, ask a stone mason to let you have little pieces of polished and unpolished granite to look at. What differences between them can you see?

A granite-faced building

7 Grow crystals As we have seen, when the lava from a volcano cools down, often beautiful shapes called crystals are formed.

You can make some crystals of your own if you add salt to some warm water in a clean jam-jar. Stir the salt until it dissolves. Keep adding salt to the water until no more will dissolve. You have now made a strong or concentrated salt solution.

Pour a little of the salt solution into a clean saucer and leave it on the windowsill. When all the water has evaporated, look with a hand lens or magnifying glass at the crystals left in the saucer. What do you notice about them?

If you want to make big crystals, evaporate your salt solution very slowly.

Make some more crystals in the same way. Try sugar, washing soda, alum, lemonade powder, and Epsom salts. Alum and Epsom salts can be bought quite cheaply from a chemist's shop.

8 The growth of a volcano Draw a series of coloured pictures showing how a volcano might grow from being a hole in the ground to becoming a high mountain. Make sure you put in lots of smoke in big grey clouds and red-hot lava in streaming ribbons. You could put your volcano next to the sea.

42

9 The mystery of the new volcano Pretend that one day you are out for a walk in a lonely part of the country. Suddenly you feel the ground beneath your feet rumbling and shaking. From a crack in a nearby rock you see smoke and sparks drifting upwards. Have you discovered a new volcano?

Write a story about your adventures. Describe what the countryside is like, what you see, how you feel, and what you do.

Can you think of a funny explanation for the ground rumbling and shaking, and for the smoke and sparks coming from the rocks? Include this in your story.

10 A model underwater volcano Make a model underwater volcano. You will need a small narrow-necked bottle, a wide glass jar, some ink or food colouring, and some string.

Tie the string to the small bottle. Fill the jar with cold water. Put a few drops of ink or food colouring in the small bottle and then fill it with hot water (*Careful!*)

Lower the bottle quickly by the string to the bottom of the jar. A cloud of coloured water will rise out of the bottle, rather like a volcano, and will spread to the surface of the cold water in the jar. The hot water rises because it is lighter than cold water.

11 Make some toffee

Just as volcanic lava cools and solidifies to form rock, so liquid toffee can be cooled to form a solid. Like igneous rocks, toffee sometimes has crystals (of sugar) in it.

You will need:
175g butter
225g soft brown sugar
225g golden syrup
1 small tin (200g) condensed milk
A greased baking tin, about 28 × 18 cms
A grown-up to help you

What you do:

1 Melt the butter in a large saucepan

2 Add the sugar and syrup and heat *gently* to dissolve the sugar.

3 Stir until it boils and add the condensed milk.

4 Boil steadily for about 20 minutes, stirring all the time with a wooden spoon. The mixture will thicken and go to a golden colour.

5 Drop a small amount of the mixture into a saucer of cold water. If the toffee is ready it should form a soft, round ball. If not, continue heating for a little longer.

6 Carefully pour the molten toffee into the greased tin and leave it to solidify. Then break it into pieces.

Do remember to clean your teeth after eating this toffee.

12 Make a wallchart Collect
pictures of volcanic scenery. Make a
wallchart or scrapbook with your pictures.
Write a sentence or two about each of the
pictures.

13 Disappearing islands As we
saw in the case of Surtsey (page 33),
sometimes a new island appears when a
volcano erupts under the sea. Sometimes,
though, the island later disappears. One
volcanic island off the coast of Alaska has
appeared and disappeared several times in
the last 200 years. Write a story called 'The
Disappearing Island'. Describe your
adventures in searching for, and finding,
this island.

14 Make a book Make a book.
Describe all the things we use rocks for.
Collect as many interesting pictures as you
can to illustrate your book. Draw some
pictures of your own.

15 A model volcanic island Make
a model volcanic island. Perhaps you could
make a model of Tristan da Cunha (see
page 30).
   You will need a cardboard tube about 10
centimetres long and a large piece of
cardboard or hardboard. Stick the tube
down to the cardboard or hardboard with
Sellotape. Mound up clay, plasticine or
papier mâché around the tube to make the
volcano's cone and the shape of your
island.
   Paint your model when it is dry. You can
make realistic-looking 'lava' by mixing
some red or orange paint with a little glue
or paste. Slowly and carefully pour this
mixture on top of the cone of the volcano so
that it runs down the sides. Make some tiny
houses to stick down on your volcanic
island. You could also include some sea,
and put some people escaping in boats
from the island!

Things to find out

1 Here are the names of some active or dormant volcanoes which were not mentioned in this book:
Lassen Peak
Mount Ngauruhoe
Lengai
San Benedicto
Hekla
Tambora
Find out in which countries these volcanoes are to be found. How high is each? When did each of these volcanoes last erupt?

2 Find out where volcanic or igneous rocks are found in your country. What is the landscape like in these places?

3 The rocks in the picture are made of granite. They were once deep underground. How do you think these rocks came to be on the surface now? Why are they such strange shapes?

Staples Tor, Dartmoor National Park

4 When the hot water from volcanoes is used by people it is sometimes called geothermal power. Try to find out what the word 'geothermal' really means.

5 Why are igneous rocks often used for making roads and in buildings?

6 Similar to geysers, but much weaker, are hot springs. Hot water trickles from underground in these springs. In some parts of the world such as Britain, France and Japan, the hot water is used to treat certain illnesses. Find out exactly where and how these hot springs are used. What illnesses are treated at the hot springs?

7 Find out all you can about vineyards. What is grown in a vineyard? How is the crop looked after? What is done with it? Why are there often vineyards on the slopes of volcanoes?

8 Why are granite, limestone and sandstone used for quite different purposes? What makes each one particularly suitable for these different purposes?

9 Why would you not expect to find fossils in igneous rocks?

10 Can you find any evidence of past or present volcanic activity near to where you live?

11 Pumice is one rock which is sometimes formed when lava from a volcano cools and hardens. Occasionally pumice becomes a hazard to shipping. Find out why this should be.

12 Find out how pieces of rock and cinders from a volcano might be turned into soil.

Glossary

Here are the meanings of some words which you might have met for the first time in this book.

Block mountains: flattish-topped mountains formed where a large block of land has been pushed up between two roughly parallel faults.

Caldera: a very wide hollow which is formed when the cone of a volcano explodes, collapses or wears away. Often a lake forms in the caldera when the volcano becomes extinct.

Composite cone: the most common kind of volcano: a conical hill or mountain built up by many eruptions of lava alternating with layers of ash and cinders. It is also called a stratovolcano.

Cone: the hill or mound of volcanic materials that is built up around the opening of a volcano.

Continent: one of the large pieces of land on the Earth's surface.

Core: the centre of the Earth which is made of the metals iron and nickel. The inner core is thought to be solid, the outer core a liquid.

Crater: the cup-shaped hollow around the opening of a volcano.

Crust: the Earth's outer layer of rock on which we live.

Crystals: the strange and beautiful shapes into which minerals and some other chemical substances grow.

Dormant: a term used to describe a volcano which is 'resting' or 'sleeping', and which has not erupted in recent years.

Earthquake: a movement or tremor of the Earth's crust, often caused where the Earth's plates move against each other.

Epicentre: the point on the Earth's surface immediately above the spot where an earthquake occurs.

Eruption: the forcing of lava and other volcanic material out of a weak spot in the Earth's crust.

Extinct: a term used to describe a volcano which has not erupted for thousands of years.

Fault: a large crack or break in a series of rocks. The rocks on one or both sides of the fault may slip up or down.

Fold: the bending of rocks caused by movements of the Earth's surface.

Fold mountains: mountains that have been pushed up into huge folds or ridges by movements of the Earth's surface.

Fossil: the remains of a plant or animal that has been buried and preserved for a long time in rocks of the Earth's crust.

Geyser: a spring that from time to time throws a jet of hot water and steam into the air.

Igneous rocks: rocks that have solidified from volcanic lava.

Lava: the molten rock that comes out of a volcano.

Mantle: the layer of rock below the Earth's crust and above the core. The mantle is believed to be so hot that some of the rocks have melted and are a liquid.

Pangaea: the vast continent that was once formed millions of years ago from all the Earth's present-day continents.

Plate: one of the sections of the Earth's crust. The slow but steady movements of the plates cause changes in the Earth's surface.

Rift valley: a steep-sided valley formed when a block of land slips down between two roughly parallel faults.

Shield volcano: a volcano formed from runny lava. It is shaped like an upturned shield or saucer.

Spring: a flow of water from the ground, formed from rainwater which has sunk into the ground.

Stratovolcano: see composite cone.

Tsunami: the large sea wave, sometimes called a tidal wave, caused by an earthquake or volcanic eruption on the sea-bed.

Volcano: a hole or tear at a weak spot in the Earth's crust from which gases and molten rock (lava) flow. A hill or mountain may form around this hole or tear.

Index